GREAT
PHILOSOPHERS

Consulting Editors
Ray Monk and Frederic Raphael

Raymond Plant

....

HEGEL

On Religion and Philosophy

PHŒNIX

A PHOENIX PAPERBACK

First published in Great Britain in 1997 by
Phoenix, a division of the Orion Publishing Group Ltd
Orion House
5 Upper Saint Martin's Lane
London, WC2H 9EA

A catalogue reference for this book is available
from the British Library.

ISBN 0 753 80185 X

Typeset by Deltatype Ltd, Birkenhead, Merseyside

Printed in Great Britain by
Clays Ltd, St Ives plc

For Iris Murdoch

Philosophers are doomed to find Hegel waiting patiently at the end of whatever road we travel.

(Richard Porty)

Hegelianism only extends its historical domination, finally unfolding its immense enveloping resources without obstacle.

(Jacques Derrida)

HEGEL

On Philosophy and Religion

THE IMPORTANCE OF HEGEL

Hegel is a pivotally important figure in the history of western philosophy and his work was immensely wide-ranging. It was and is still pervasively influential in a wide number of fields: in the central areas of philosophy itself; in political and social theory; in aesthetics; in the philosophy of history; and in theology and the philosophy of religion, which is the basic theme of this book. Philosophers working in these fields are, even today, very often involved in taking stock of Hegel's own thinking and in articulating their own thought in relation to his. Major thinkers in this century from a wide range of traditions in philosophy are scarcely comprehensible without understanding their relation to Hegel. This is true of Sartre, Heidegger, Merleau Ponty, Kojève (whose thought has been reworked by Francis Fukuyama in his writing on the 'end of history'), Derrida, Lacan, Rorty, Royce, Althusser, Charles Taylor, Adorno, Marcuse, Fromm, and many others. In the nineteenth century, F.C. Baur Feuerbach, Strauss, Marx, Kierkegaard, Nietzsche, T.H. Green – all worked in the shadow of Hegel.

In this book, however, we shall be concerned mainly with Hegel's contribution to religious thought and again here his influence is profound. Karl Löwith in *From Hegel to Nietzsche: The Revolution in Nineteenth Century Thought*, described Hegel as *the* philosopher of the bourgeois Christian world and while, as Karl Barth argued in *Nineteenth*

Century Religious Thought, he did not quite become the Aquinas of Protestantism, nevertheless his thought exercised a profound influence on those who followed him. His immediate followers, for example Strauss in *The Life of Jesus* and Feuerbach in *The Essence of Christianity*, took up and radicalized Hegelian themes. Marx was deeply indebted to Hegel even though he became a stern critic. In the work of Kierkegaard we see the impact of a severe reaction to Hegel's philosophy of religion particularly in *Either/Or*; and in Nietzsche too, particularly in his reflections on the 'death of God'. Marx, Kierkegaard and Nietzsche in very different ways destroyed the idea of unity between God and humanity which had been at the centre of Hegel's thought. In Britain his religious thought became profoundly salient in the work of the British Idealists such as T. H. Green, Sir Henry Jones, Bernard Bosanquet, and John and Edward Caird. They in their turn influenced those who wrote *Lux Mundi* edited by Charles Gore, one of the most significant works of late nineteenth-century theology. Gore himself, a bishop in the Anglican Church, was profoundly influenced by Hegel, both in general and in his understanding of the Eucharist, as his book, *The Body of Christ*, shows. In this century Hegel's work was a major influence on the 'Death of God' theologians such as Hamilton and Altizer; on the post-modern theology of Mark Taylor, and on the work of J. Moltmann and Dorothee Sölle, important German theologians. Equally, Hegel has been a profound influence on two of the greatest theologians of this century: Wolfhart Pannenberg, whose book *Jesus: God and Man* grapples with Hegel's thought on Christology, and Hans Küng, the Tübingen theologian, who wrote *The Incarnation of God* which is devoted to an examination of Hegel's theology. So there can be no doubting the enormous impact of Hegel's work in a wide range of fields including theology and religious thought. Indeed, it is one of the daunting facts about Hegel that he saw his own work as a systematic whole and it is not possible to detach the meaning and impact of his religious thought from all the other areas of his work in philosophy, political theory, aesthetics and history. So, while we shall concentrate on religious issues, these were not for Hegel a detachable part of his thought which has to be taken as a whole. As we go along I shall attempt to explain how his religious thought impacts on these other works.

LIFE AND DEVELOPMENT

George William Frederick Hegel was born in Stuttgart in 1770, where his father was a minor official in the court of the Duke of Württemberg. His father was ambitious for his son and he was educated at the Stuttgart Gymnasium and then the Tübingen Stift, the famous Swabian theological seminary, which he duly entered in 1788 with a view to studying theology and becoming either a Lutheran pastor or a member of the *Honorationen* who would administer the state.

At the Tübingen Stift, situated in idyllic surroundings on the bank of the Neckar, he shared a room with the poet Hölderlin and with the mercurial Schelling whose development as a philosopher was precocious. At the seminary this small band studied the usual range of theological and philosophical subjects. They welcomed the French Revolution by planting a liberty tree on the outskirts of the town. Indeed the degree of political radicalism in the Stift alarmed the Duke who made formal visitations, one of which was a theme in Peter Weiss's play *Hölderlin*. More importantly for their later development, they all shared a sense of the fragmentation and divisions which they believed afflicted modern culture. In particular they were concerned with the division or bifurcation between God and man; man and nature, and man and society. It was in this developing vision that the ideas of alienation and estrangement which so characterized not only their own subsequent work, but also influenced Marx and subsequent humanistic Marxists such as Fromm and Marcuse, were first to be found.

After graduating from the Stift Hegel declined to go into the ministry of the church or the Duke and took a post as house tutor in Bern. Hegel was very miserable in Bern although he enjoyed walking around the lake, as Rousseau had done, but he was oppressed by the tedium of bourgeois life and he was delighted, after a relatively short time in Bern, by a move to Frankfurt where his friend Hölderlin lived. In Frankfurt he wrote more than he did in Bern and, as we shall see, those writings, along with those in Bern, form the basis of what have been published as his *Early Theological Writings*. These include extended essays on *The Positivity of the Christian Religion*; *The Life of Jesus*; *The Spirit of Christianity and Its Fate*; together with a short essay *On Love* and the profoundly interesting, albeit fragmentary, *Earliest System – Programme of German Idealism*.

The death of Hegel's father in 1799 left him with a small legacy which enabled him to contemplate becoming a *Privatdocent* at the University of Jena where his friend, Schelling, was a Professor of Philosophy. The post was unsalaried and he depended on student fees and it was not until Goethe intervened, having received representations from Hegel, that he was eventually given a salaried post.

Nevertheless, it was in Jena that Hegel was able to bring his thought together for the first time and he produced lectures which were to form the system of his philosophy which he was to refine and develop more fully later. He was also able to write *The Phenomenology of Spirit* which was to form an introduction to his systematic philosophy and is one of the most profoundly important books in modern western philosophy. The book was completed in trying circumstances. Napoleon had laid siege to Jena and the manuscript of the book was carried to his publisher in Bamberg by a rider who went through the French lines. At this stage of his life Hegel was an admirer of Napoleon. As we saw, he had welcomed the French Revolution with his friends in the Tübingen Stift but had become very disillusioned with the advent of the Terror. He saw Napoleon as embodying the rational and modernizing principles of the Revolution while at the same time curbing its excesses.

The arrival of Napoleon, however, spelled the end of Hegel's career in Jena since the university closed and he had to look for another post; he became editor of the *Bamberg Gazette*, a Catholic paper. Although Hegel seems to have enjoyed his period as editor during this politically pivotal time, he was not destined to last long in the position. His friend and patron Niethammer had become an important figure in Bavarian education charged with the duty of transforming the curriculum of the schools into a modern humanistic form and reducing the dominance of the Catholic Church in education. In 1808 he offered Hegel the post of Rector of the Grammar School in Nuremberg. This was a post that Hegel was to hold until 1816. During this period he wrote *The Philosophical Propaedeutic* which was in some ways a simplified version of his system which he had developed in Jena so that it could be used as a basis for philosophical instruction in the school. This *Propaedeutic* covered Logic; the Philosophy of Nature; the Philosophy of Mind, or what he called Subjective Spirit; the Philosophy of Objective Spirit – the science of law, morals and religion;

and the Philosophy of Absolute Spirit, which was concerned with the relationship between philosophy, art and religion. During the time he spent in Nuremberg he wrote *The Science of Logic*, one of the few books he was actually to publish himself. This book, together with *The Phenomenology of Spirit*, led to Hegel being offered a chair in philosophy in Heidelberg in 1816. In Heidelberg his greatest achievement was to write and publish his *Encyclopaedia of the Philosophical Sciences* which further enhanced his reputation, since his Jena and Nuremberg drafts had not been published, and for the first time the German literary public could see and understand his systematic approach to philosophy.

In 1818 Hegel finally moved to the University of Berlin. He was called to Berlin at the instigation of Baron Karl Sigmund von Altenstein, who was the first minister in the newly founded ministry for educational, religious and medical affairs. Altenstein was close to the Chancellor Prince Karl August von Hardenberg and together they formed a strong reformist group within the Prussian administration. Hegel was appointed not only to the chair in philosophy but also to the Board of Examiners of the Royal Academic Board of Brandenberg and his mission was to carry out the same kind of reform of the educational curriculum in secondary schools as he had first undertaken at Niethammer's instigation in Nuremberg. Accusations levelled since that Hegel became, in some sense, the official state philosopher of Prussia have to be treated with some care. The institutions of Prussia which he defended after his appointment were those that had emerged through the reforms of Altenstein and Hardenberg. It is equally true, however, that by the time Hegel arrived in Berlin, the reform movement which had transformed Prussian society was under some pressure from the rise of Prussian nationalism. Hegel saw this nationalism, particularly in the works of Jacob Friedrich Fries, as a form of resurgent subjective romanticism of which he was severely critical. This kind of subjectivism is criticized in *The Philosophy of Right* which Hegel published during his Berlin professorship and which deals with the central issues of political philosophy: the nature of rights, property, morality, the development of the market economy, the role of marriage and the family in civil society, the role of corporations, the function of the state and the role of constitutional monarchy within it. There was a period of reaction that set in after 1821 and Hegel did ·have to accommodate himself to it as an employee of the state. Equally, there is no doubt that his own intellectual conviction was in favour of the kind of state which Hardenberg and Altenstein had tried to develop before the reaction.

Hegel died suddenly in November 1831 of either cholera or possibly stomach cancer and is buried alongside Fichte in the Dorotheenstädt Friedhof, a place of great peace and beauty.

FEARS OF FRAGMENTATION

As I pointed out in the last section, during his time at the Tübingen Stift, Hegel, Hölderlin and Schelling were preoccupied with what they saw as deep problems of division and fragmentation in modern life and in particular the bifurcation between man and God; between man and society, between man and nature, and indeed the division within the individual's own personality between reason, imagination and feeling, and they gave their diagnosis of these forms of bifurcation and fragmentation a religious basis. Before turning to their account of these forms of estrangement, however, it is worth saying something about the intellectual context in which these fears arose. In the late eighteenth century there had been a major rediscovery of the importance of classical Greece in German culture. This rediscovery covered all aspects of Greek life and in particular the culture of the city state or *polis* in its religious, moral, artistic and poetic forms. It seemed that the Greek city state exhibited an ideal of the unity of life: religion was integrated into the daily life of the society and the family; the religion was not over-intellectualized – the performance of religious duties involved the emotions and imagination as well as the intellect; the society embodied a sense of common purpose and a sense of community – and this was again partly due to the fact that it was integrated by common religious beliefs; men and nature lived more fully in harmony – and again this was in large part due to the ways in which religion coloured attitudes to nature. Two good examples of this idealization of the Greek *polis* are to be found in two very influential figures in the generation before Hegel, namely Schiller and Herder. In his poem *The Gods of Greece*, Schiller points out how closely the different aspects of Greek life were interwoven and how crucial a common religious life was to securing this common life and sense of community. These themes were set out even more fully in his *Letters on the Aesthetic Education of Man*. In this work the unity of Greek life and experience is used as a foil to the diagnosis of what Schiller took to be the almost opposite trends in modern German culture. The same point is made by Herder in his monumental *Auch eine Philosophie der Geschichte zur Bildung der Menschheit* published in 1774. In this book Herder dwelled on the ways in which Greek forms of experience had enabled man to maximize his potentialities and powers, to be a whole man. In contrast, his own times seemed to him to have lost sight of some of the most valuable of human qualities. Greece was the glorious youth of the human race; now society was fragmented. In his *Denkmal Johann Winckelmans* he argues for what he calls 'the rebirth of the Greek Spirit in Germany'.

Hegel and Hölderlin were inspired by this vision of the unity of all things within the ancient *polis* and were equally convinced of the multiple types of fragmentation in modern European and in particular German culture. This was a major theme in Hölderlin's *Hyperion* which he began to write at the Stift. The forms of bifurcation with which they were concerned, though, went far beyond this. There was the divorce between man and God to be found, as they

12

saw it, in conventional Christianity in which God, in the Judaeo/Christian tradition, is wholly other and universal and thus rather indifferent to the ways of life of particular societies (as Rousseau had pointed out in *The Social Contract*, thus making Christianity inimical to the social spirit and the unity of society). Unlike the Greek, the Christian's home was not of this world. Indeed the impetus for the Judaeo/Christian tradition starting with Abraham as the father of the Jewish nation was a snapping of all the bonds of family, society and rootedness to place. In the book of Genesis, in Hegel's view, this trend was revealed very starkly when God said to Abraham: 'Get thee out of thy country, from thy kindred, and from thy father's house, unto a land that I will shew thee.' As Hegel says, commenting on these passages:

> With his herds Abraham wandered hither and thither over a boundless territory without bringing parts of it nearer to him by cultivating and improving them ... he was a stranger to soil and men alike ... The whole world Abraham regarded his opposite; if he did not take it to be a nullity he looked upon it as sustained by a God who was alien to it. Nothing in nature was supposed to have any part in God; everything was simply under God's mastery.[1]

These ideas had an impact on Christianity, growing as it did out of these Jewish ideas. The Christian for St Peter was like 'a pilgrim in a foreign land', which is not a sentiment that could have occurred in Greek religion in his view. As Hegel says in an essay not published until 1907: 'our religion wishes to educate men to be citizens of heaven who always look on high and this makes them strangers to human feeling.'[2] Christianity was a private religion, concerned with personal salvation, not with social and moral unity in the community as he says again in the same essay: 'Private religion forms the morality of the individual man, but the religion of the people as well as the political circumstances forms the spirit of the people.'[3] The Christian religion was highly intellectualized with theology and doctrines which in turn divided Christians, but more importantly caused dissonance in religious life since the imagination and the heart, Hegel argued, are 'sent empty away'. It was therefore essential to have the engagement of the emotions and the imagination in religion. Christianity also led to a distancing of man from nature. As Schiller had argued in *The Gods of Greece*, the Greek gods were seen by their devotees to be actively involved in the natural order. The gods were not transcendent and distant from the world. Because the divine entered into every part of their lives they were deeply at home in the natural world and the very pervasiveness of their divinities gave a unity to their social and natural lives. But, according to Schiller, this golden age has fled from the world.

From an early age, therefore, Hegel was deeply concerned with the question of the relationship between religion and a common life in society and with the potential role of religion in securing an integration of the human personality, to overcome what in *The Phenomenology of Spirit* he was to call 'the unhappy consciousness' and to have a sense of 'being at home in the world'. Some of the thinkers I have mentioned called for a restoration of something like Greek values in Germany and while Hegel was sympathetic enough to that, envisaging as it did a restoration of a sense of community and of the unity of the personality, he was equally clear that there could be no going back to Greece or changing the religious dimension of modern life to a straightforward Greek model. It was not possible to import something like Greek religion into Germany; equally there was no hope of going behind Christianity and reinstating pre-Christian Germanic forms of religion which may have played more of a part than Christianity in securing a common life as some had suggested. There could be no direct resurrection of the Greek experience of religion, partly because it was divorced from the nature of modern religious culture but also because the modern world had experienced the rise of individualism. This individualism had certainly fractured the unity of the community but had also led to many gains in the character of human experience. Any restored sense of community and integration had to take full account of the role of individualism. Greek society had a sense of what Hegel, following Schiller, called unmediated unity; any restored sense of community would have to become a form of mediated unity; that is to say, one which recognized and sought to reintegrate the modern sense of individualism.

As Hegel says, while 'Achea cannot be the Tueton's fatherland', can Judea? That is to say, can Christianity be interpreted and disseminated in such a way that it can become what religion was to the Greeks, namely a folk religion, one that will form the basis of a common life? Christianity is what we have and if religion can ever become again the focus of a common life and the unity of the self, then the Christian religion has to be transformed, and it was this transformation to which he set his hand in his writings in Bern and Frankfurt. It is important to notice, though, that at this stage he is not writing as a philosopher, seeking to set Christianity into a wider interpretation of human existence as he was later to do; rather he is acting as a kind of cultural critic seeing what scope there might be for the transformation of Christianity.

In Bern and Frankfurt he wrote two essays on these themes: *The Life of Jesus* and *The Spirit of Christianity and Its Destiny*. What is necessary to secure this transformation of Christianity is a recognition of the divine within life and within the social world which orthodox Christianity neglects. In Hegel's view in *Das Leben Jesu* it is perfectly possible to interpret the message of Jesus in this way. He points out the inadequacy of the Jews' conception of God that led to their baneful experience of alienation. Their divinity was outside them, 'unseen and unfelt', whereas the life of Jesus makes articulate in a particular case that visible, tangible relationship with God that must exist if a harmonious community of believers is to be established. This is the impact of the Incarnation which is absolutely critical for Hegel: 'if the divine is to appear, the invisible spirit must be united with something visible so that the whole may be unified ... so that there may be a completed synthesis, a perfected harmony.'[4] This was the real message of Jesus in which the Divine Father and the tangible, palpable Son are 'simply modifications of the same life'. This was the message that Jesus came to teach, that the 'Word is not far off but nigh'; in the Incarnation the divine is united to human life, human form, to history and to nature. In his own terms, though, Jesus's message was a failure. In Hegel's

16

view, in *The Spirit of Christianity and Its Destiny*, Jesus was faced with two choices, given the weight of the alternative Jewish tradition and its conception of God. Jesus's conception of the relationship between human and divine was unintelligible to the Jews. It was impossible to reform their religious beliefs from the inside; the alternative was to challenge them from the outside and this is what he did more and more, and as such his message was purely ideal and Utopian. This meant that the disciples, who were Jews, understood the nature of God and man in Jesus too much in the context of Jewish theistic ideas. Instead of following Jesus in teaching a general message about the reconciliation of the divine and the human in all life, this reconciliation was understood to be achieved in Jesus alone. So instead of the Incarnation becoming a symbol within Christianity for an achieved reconciliation between God and all humanity, the divine and human were understood to be linked only in the one life.

As I have argued, Hegel did not approach these issues in terms of having a fully developed philosophical account of human existence within which to situate his account of Christianity. Nevertheless, these early theological writings are of the greatest importance for understanding the nature of Hegel's mature approach to the philosophy of religion. The unity of the divine and the world was, at this stage, a religious intuition which he struggled to express in ways that could make it the basis of such a common life and restored humanity. Some of these ideas may seem rather strange to twentieth-century eyes, particularly to those who do not follow theological debate, so it is worth stopping at this stage briefly to indicate how some of these ideas are regarded as salient by one recent well-respected philosopher of religion. In *The Borderlands of Theology* Donald Mackinnon produces the following remarkable paragraph which bears closely on Hegel's preoccupations at this point:

> We have to reckon with elements in the tradition [of Christianity] itself which seem to encourage us to free our religious imaginations from too tight a bondage to Jesus in the days of his flesh. There is the Johannine theology of the Paraclete, and above all perhaps that obscure saying of St Paul which has so baffled exegetes (in II Corinthians) of 'knowing Christ no longer *kata sarka*' (after the flesh). Were not the Hegelians justified in construing the *Noli me tangere* of the risen Christ to Mary Magdalene in the record of the fourth Gospel as a concrete mythical expression of the demand that Christians discard the bondage of a false attachment to the details of a particular history, and adhere within themselves to a way of life which they must realise in circumstances altogether strange to those who first listened to Jesus?[5]

This provides us with a deep insight into what Hegel was getting at as his thought developed in these early theological writings. That the message of Jesus of the reconciliation of God and humanity has to be detached from his own person ('do not touch me') and that the spirit of Jesus embodying this reconciliation has to be appropriated by men and women to become the basis of a new form of community and new kind of human nature.

TOWARDS PHILOSOPHY

As his thought matured, however, Hegel moved towards setting this reinterpretation of Christianity in a much wider and dauntingly complex conceptual scheme which I shall try to outline shortly. Before moving to that task, however, one potential paradox has to be resolved in this move towards a philosophy which could provide the basis of common life and the unity of the person. After all, had not Hegel argued that rational thought had been partly the problem with Christianity? It had been turned into theology and doctrine. So how will situating Christianity within such a conceptual framework help? If theology and doctrine 'send the imagination and heart empty away', will not philosophy do the same? In so far as there is a way of resolving this paradox, it has to be found in Hegel's fragmentary work *The Earliest System – Programme of German Idealism*, in which he argues as follows:

> Here I shall discuss an idea which, as far as I know has not occurred to anyone else – we must have a new mythology, but this mythology must be in the service of the Ideas, it must be a mythology of Reason. Until we express the Ideas aesthetically, i.e. mythologically, they have no interest for the people, and conversely until mythology is rational the philosopher must be ashamed of it. Thus in the end enlightened and unenlightened must clasp hands, mythology must become philosophi-

cal in order to make the people rational and philosophy must become mythological in order to make philosophers sensible (*sinnlich*). Then reigns eternal unity among us. No more the look of scorn of the enlightened philosopher looking down on the mob, no more the blind trembling of the people before its wise men and priests. Then first awaits us equal development of all powers, of what is peculiar to each and what is common to all. No power shall any longer be suppressed for universal freedom and equality of spirits will reign – A higher spirit sent from heaven must found this new religion among us. It will be the last and greatest work of mankind.[6]

A new 'mythology' is essential to form the basis of a common life, but if this set of common understandings is to be available to all it must combine both reason and feeling so that imagination and heart are not sent empty away. If philosophy is to fulfil this role, as Hegel comes to believe that it can, it must speak in a new idiom which will combine both reason and lived experience. This remains the case whether that experience is religious, of one's own basic psychological states and instincts, of one's historical identity, of one's rooted moral experience, of one's dealings with nature, or of one's aesthetic and poetic sense. All of these have to be incorporated into a new kind of philosophy by which they will be reinterpreted and transformed, to make the basis of a new 'mythology' and of common life. Hegel wrote this piece in 1796 and by 1801 he had made considerable progress in developing a new philosophical perspective. By that time he was able to write, in his essay on *The Difference between Fichte's and Schelling's Systems of Philosophy*, that 'bifurcation is the source of the need for philosophy.' It is to philosophy that he now looks for the basis of a harmonious interpretation of experience within which some of the ideas about religion which he had developed in Bern and Frankfurt will be set into a new context.

What conditions does philosophy have to meet in order to provide this interpretation of human experience and existence of which religion is a part? First of all it has to be comprehensive and systematic. It has to be comprehensive in that it has to deal with all the major forms of human experience and activity and with the basic psychological structures of the selves who engage in such activities. These cannot be separated off in a clear-cut way. The nature of the self and its capacities has to be understood, at least in part, in relation to the basic forms of activity in which humans engage: familial, economic, political, artistic, religious and philosophical. While it is possible to describe the basic structures of human psychology and the components of selfhood, he argues that such a theory of mind separated from an account of the major forms of experience and activity in which human selves develop their powers will be one-sided and rationalistic in the ways that he criticized in the passage from *The Earliest System – Programme of German Idealism*. As he later argues, criticizing a purely abstract approach to the nature of the self: 'the Ego is by itself only a formal identity ... Consciousness appears differently modified according to the difference of the given object and the

21

gradual specification of consciousness appears as a variation in the characteristics of the objects.'[7]

Human beings only develop a rich sense of selfhood in relation to common activities. There they achieve recognition from others and by engagement with the world both natural and social. So a unified theory of the mind has to relate an account of the basic structures of mentality with the types of activities in which people engage. This point has been put in a modern idiom by Stuart Hampshire in *Thought and Action*, a brilliant book within the analytical tradition of philosophy which has often showed deep antipathy for Hegel, but which illustrates the salience of the views of Hegel we are now discussing:

> philosophy of mind will be a theory of the order of the development of human powers with their corresponding virtues and not a theory of their unchanging constitution. Metaphysical deduction may be replaced by a study of the successive forms of social life and the typical processes by which one form of social life, with its corresponding moral ideas is typically transformed into another.[8]

This necessary link between an account of the mind and the modes of its realization will satisfy one of Hegel's demands for philosophy to be closer to actual experience in the different modes of social life: religious, familial, social, economic, political, artistic.

Their second requirement is that philosophy should be systematic. It has to provide an account of all the basic modes of social life and their inconnectedness if the ideal of a unified society and a unified conception of humanity is to be attained. It is Hegel's firm view, in his mature writings, that beneath the surface differences between the various activities in which human beings are engaged there is an underlying connectedness which can be brought to the surface by philosophy in a systematic, conceptual manner. In this, his approach is fundamentally different from that of post-modern philosophers who not only recognize the discontinuities and forms of diremption which Hegel saw it as his mission to overcome, but actually revel in these discontinuities. In the view of Lyotard for example, there is and can be no philosophical 'meta narrative' which will provide an interpretation of all the forms of human experience and locate them in their appropriate place in the development of human powers. In this sense, the approach of post-modern thinkers who emphasize, and indeed celebrate, the fragmentation of human life and thought are profoundly anti-Hegelian.

In adopting this systematic view, Hegel equally poses a major challenge to those philosophers in the analytical tradition nurtured on Wittgenstein. They argue that we are faced with a range of different language games, each with its own logic and each embodying different human interests. These language games are incommensurable. There is no overarching conception of reason since what is rational and irrational is internal to specific language games and the specific human interests they embody. The cost of this sort of fragmentation of reason for Hegel is the loss of a sense of the unity of the self and the unity of society. The self becomes dissipated in a set of different and irreconcilable language games or first-order narratives.

For Hegel philosophy also has to be historical. Given that

the nature of the human mind and its development have to be considered in relation to the modes of social existence, these modes cannot just be taken as given. Their development has to be understood along with the evolution of the powers of the mind. The concepts in terms of which we characterize our religious, aesthetic, social and political lives are not just abstract and universal, although they do have these elements. They are also to be understood in developmental terms, too. So for Hegel 'The shapes that the concept assumes in the course of its actualisation are indispensable for the knowledge of the concept itself.' This historical development is teleological – that is to say it is a rational process towards an overarching end which is the attainment of what he calls Absolute Knowledge. This is the state attained when all the shapes of human life, in terms of both their historical development and their interconnectedness, are fully understood. This historical process is full of difficulties and contingencies which have to be comprehended. Hegel, in *The Phenomenology of Spirit*, compares this development to the Via Dolorosa and Golgotha, but, as with the agony, death and resurrection of Christ, there is redemption when this process is fully comprehended:

> The goal, Absolute Knowing, or spirit that knows itself as Spirit, has for its path the recollection of the Spirits (that is, the different forms of human experience in history and their organising principles or ethos RP) as they are in themselves and as they accomplish the organisation of their realm. Their preservation, regarded from the side of their free existence (that is, not set within a structure of philosophical explanation RP) appearing in the form of

contingency, is History; but regarded from the side of their philosophically comprehended organisation, it is the science of Knowing in the sphere of appearance: the two together, comprehended History, form alike the inwardising and the Calvary of absolute Spirit.[9]

When we understand this history of the basic modes of human experience we have reached the level of Absolute Knowledge, but there are two further elements to the picture which need to be addressed. Both have to do with the nature of the teleological development at stake here.

History for Hegel, as is obvious from the above, is not 'one damn thing after another', a series of discontinuous contingent events. There is a structure to this development. Part of this structure is given by the idea of *dialectic*. This is a concept in Hegel on which a very great deal of ink has been spilled and this is not the place for a full analysis and appraisal. Suffice it to say that the process of dialectic is the process in which an account of how forms of life develop is embodied. Forms of social life, whether religious, political, artistic or social, have organizing principles or forms of ethos. The process of dialectical development shows how in human history one form turns into another because contradictions are revealed in previous forms. Previous forms are not lost in the dialectical development. Rather what is true in them, in the sense of the realization of some basic human capacity or meeting some basic need, is carried over into a richer and deeper form of life which both incorporates and transcends and goes beyond what has gone before. This process is not accidental or contingent, but can be understood and grasped philosophically. We often do not manage this because we remain stranded at the level of what Hegel calls the 'Understanding', in which things are looked at for what they are in themselves and not in relationship to each other. The level of the Understanding (*Vorstellung*) is indispensable, but it has to be transcended to arrive at the level of Reason, where there is a full conceptual (*Begriff*) grasp of things in their interrelatedness. So dialectic, in recording the internal development of forms of life from one to the other, is also the passage from the Understanding to Reason, but going back to Hegel's earlier strictures on the role of Reason, because it incorporates history and experience, is not a kind of universalist abstraction.

The second philosophically important point about the development of historical experience is that it is not accidental. There is rather a deep rationality at work which the philosopher uncovers on the road to Absolute Knowledge. This rationality is secured because there is something analogous to the action of God united with human life and history whose action is the basis for the rationality of the process. I said 'something analogous to God' because in his philosophical work, particularly in *The Science of Logic*, Hegel calls this conception the *Absolute Idea*, that is to say the organizing principle of human existence which becomes concrete in the world of nature, in the world of history and human society and in art, religion and philosophy. As the *Absolute Idea* is embodied in diverse but comprehensibly connected forms of human experience, it becomes Spirit. When fully comprehended philosophically it is *Absolute Spirit*. At the level of the Understanding, or in everyday experience in a Christian society, this process is understood as God creating the world and Jesus as the incarnate son of God being God identified with human life. The level of Absolute Knowledge is the philosophical transcription of the doctrine of the Holy Spirit mediating in religious terms between the Father and the Son. At the Absolute level of Knowledge this is interpreted in conceptual terms as carrying within us, in a public and rationally defensible way, an understanding of the deep unity of human life and experience. So to put it simply: God as he is in himself before the foundation of the world is transformed by Hegel into the Absolute Idea. The philosophical understanding of the rationality of human experience and history is equivalent to the incarnate life of God, or the embodiment of the Absolute Idea, linking the divine to the human in everyday life and experience. Absolute Knowledge is the transcription of the religious idea of the role of the Holy Spirit when we have a comprehensive understanding of the indwelling of God in this process. Hegel's philosophy therefore provides a deep interpretation of the Trinity:

> The first moment is the idea in its simple universality for itself, self-enclosed, having not yet progressed to the primal division, to otherness – the Father. The second is the particular, the idea in appearance – the Son. It is the idea in its externality, such that the external appearance is converted back to the first [moment] and is known as the divine idea, the identity of the divine and the human. The third element, then, is this consciousness – God as the Spirit. The Spirit as existing and realizing itself is the community.[10]

It is Hegel's claim that his philosophy embodies this standpoint. So, as we can see, Hegel sets religion in the context of a full account of human life and existence and in so doing transcends religion by philosophy. It gets away from the symbols, the parables, the picture thinking of religion which depends for its authority on subjective faith and which has misrepresented itself in the ways that we looked at earlier, in favour of a rational system of understanding human existence which, because it is rational, is open to all to understand and depends upon Reason and not faith. Religion is an indispensable stepping stone to Absolute Knowledge, but it does have to be transcended by philosophy. At the same time, Hegel's claim is that his philosophy is a true transcription of the essence of Christianity when we detach the message of Jesus from his own life and history, although we are led to an understanding of that universal message by that life and history, which takes us back to the point made earlier by Donald Mackinnon. So, philosophy is rooted in but transcends beliefs widely held in society but at the level of common-sense understanding. In the final section I shall dwell shortly on several themes from Hegel's account of the nature of Christianity which he believes makes this claim plausible however much it leads him away from orthodoxy. We can, however, see why it is salient to see Hegel as a great Christian philosopher because Christianity is at the heart of his philosophy, albeit in this transcribed way, and in this transcribed way Christianity is turned from something that he had believed was inimical to a common life to something that could underpin and sustain it. Philosophy, in a sense, does not tell us anything new. It provides, rather, a deep account of the forms of experience and the institutions we inhabit. This vision was well captured by T. S. Eliot who was profoundly influenced by the British Hegelian philosopher, F. H. Bradley:

> We shall not cease from exploration,
> And the end of our exploring
> Shall be to arrive where we started
> And know the place for the first time.[11]

RELIGION

I have attempted to show how central religion was in Hegel's concerns and I shall now turn to some specific issues in his philosophy of religion which are illustrated in the accompanying texts. I shall concentrate on: the concept of God and our knowledge of God; the creation; the Incarnation; the Fall; and religion and philosophy.

The Concept of God

There are two things of fundamental importance in the texts in relation to this issue. He rejects the idea that it is impossible to say something determinate and true about the nature of God because of our own finitude and God's infinity. In rejecting this view in the text quoted, he is criticizing Kant, Jacobi and his Berlin colleague Schleiermacher.

In the rational theology of more recent times the principal role is played by this way of looking at things, bringing reason into the lists against itself and combatting philosophy on the grounds that reason can have no cognition of God. The consequence is that no meaning for the expression 'God' remains in theology any more than in philosophy, save only the representation, definition, or abstraction of the supreme being – a vacuum of abstraction, a vacuum of 'the beyond'. Such is the overall result of rational theology, this generally negative tendency toward any content at all in regard to the nature of God. The 'reason' of this kind of theology has in fact been nothing but abstract understanding masquerading under the name of reason, and it has ventured as far in this field as has the reason that claimed the possibility of cognition for itself. The result is that one only knows in general *that* God is: but otherwise this supreme being is inwardly empty and dead. It is not to be grasped as a living God, as concrete content; it is not to be grasped as spirit. If 'spirit' is not an empty word, then God must [be grasped] under this characteristic, just as in the church theology of former times God was called 'triune'. This is the key by which the nature of spirit is explicated. God is thus grasped as what he is for himself within himself; God [the Father] makes himself an object for himself (the Son), then, in this object, God remains the undivided essence within this differentiation of himself within himself, and in this differentiation of himself loves himself, i.e., remains identical with himself – this is God as Spirit. Hence if we are to speak of God as spirit, we must grasp God with this very definition, which exists in the church in this childlike mode of representation as the relationship between father and son – a representation that is not yet a matter of concept. Thus it is just this definition of God by the church as a Trinity that is the concrete determination and nature of God as spirit; and spirit is an empty word if it is not grasped in this determination.

But when modern theology says that we cannot have cognition of God or that God has no further determinations within himself, it knows only that God *is* as

31

something abstract without content, and in this way God is reduced to this hollow abstraction. It is all the same whether we say we cannot have cognition of God, or that God is only a supreme being. Inasmuch as we know [only] *that* God is, God is the *abstractum*. To cognize God means to have a definite, concrete concept of God. As merely having being, God is something abstract; when [God is] cognized, however, we have a representation with a content. If the representation to the effect that God is not to be cognized were substantiated through biblical exegesis, then precisely on that account we would have to turn to another source in order to arrive at a content in regard to God.[12]

The argument of the critics as Hegel sees it is that we can say no more about God's nature than that he is, and that this sense of the being of God is immediately present to consciousness. Hegel, however, rejects this view for two closely interconnected reasons. First of all we can only think and speak of God existing as a conscious being. But what do we mean by consciousness? We can only ascribe consciousness to God based on our understanding of ourselves as conscious beings and, as I pointed out earlier, for Hegel consciousness involves encounter with otherness; that is to say engagement with and recognition by what one is not. So God, as a conscious being, has this inner necessity, as all conscious beings do, to externalize himself in nature and in human life – that is to say in otherness – and through this process of externalization to come to full consciousness. As Hegel puts the point in *The Philosophy of Nature*: 'The divine Idea is just this: to disclose itself, to posit the Other outside itself and to take it back again into itself in order to be subjectivity and spirit.'[13]

Given that consciousness, including the consciousness of God, requires this engagement with otherness it follows that an understanding of the 'other' in which God is embodied, namely the world of nature and human history in its manifold forms, is itself a study of the nature of God.

Then God or spirit is this judgment [or primal division]; expressed concretely, this is the creation of the world and of the subjective spirit for which God is object. Spirit is an absolute manifesting. Its manifesting is a positing of determination and a being for an other. 'Manifesting' means 'creating an other', and indeed the creating of subjective spirit for which the absolute is. The making or creation of the world is God's self-manifesting, self-revealing. In a further and later definition we will have this manifestation in the higher form that what God creates God himself is, that in general it does not have the determinateness of an other, that God is manifestation of his own self, that God is for himself – the other (which has the empty semblance of [being] an other but is immediately reconciled), the Son of God or human being according to the divine image. Here for the first time we have consciousness, the subjectively knowing spirit for which God is object.

From this it follows that God can be known or cognised, for it is God's nature to reveal himself, to be manifest. Those who say that God is not revelatory do not speak from the [standpoint of the] Christian religion at any rate, for the Christian religion is called the

33

revealed religion. Its content is that God is revealed to human beings, that they know what God is.[14]

As Hegel says: 'God is not to be considered in isolation, for that is not possible. One knows of God only in connection with consciousness', and, as he also says, that spirit is 'self manifesting'. This all follows from the nature of consciousness as we experience it ourselves and this experience is linked to that of externalization and engagement with 'otherness'.

Creation

The inner necessity of consciousness to manifest and externalize itself in the 'other' leads us fairly naturally to Hegel's account of creation. In Hegel's view one of the defects of classical theism is that it does treat God as separate from the world and that all his attributes are as they are independent of the world. This point was well made in this century by Karl Barth in *Church Dogmatics,* vol. 3, when he argued that 'God would be no less God even if the work of creation had never been, if there were no creatures ... Hence, there can be no place for this doctrine in that of the Being of God.' Hegel rejects such a view since it makes it very difficult to understand creation as other than an entirely whimsical act on the part of God. If God had no need to create the world, if there was no inner necessity for it for the nature of God, then why did he create the world other than through whimsy? Or as he puts it in his own inimitable style in *The Philosophy of Nature*:

If God is all sufficient and lacks nothing, how does He

come to release Himself into something so clearly unequal to Him? The divine Idea is just this self-release, the expulsion of this other out of itself, and the acceptance of it again, in order to constitute subjectivity and spirit. The philosophy of nature itself belongs to this pathway of return, for it is the philosophy of nature which overcomes the division of nature and spirit, and renders to spirit the recognition of its essence in nature. This then is the position of nature within the whole; its determinateness lies in the self-determination of the Idea, by which it posits difference, another, within itself, whole maintaining infinite good in its indivisibility, and imparting its entire content in what it provides for this otherness. God disposes therefore, while remaining equal to Himself; each of these moments is itself the whole Idea, and must be posited as the divine totality. Distinctiveness can be grasped in three forms; the universal, the particular, and the singular; firstly it is preserved in the eternal unity of the Idea, the eternal son of God, as it was to *Philo*. The other of this extreme is singularity, the form of finite spirit. Singularity, as return into self, is certainly spirit, but as otherness to the exclusion of everything else, it is finite or human spirit, for we are not concerned with finite spirits other than men. In so far as the individual man is at the same time received into the unity of divine essence, he is object of the Christian religion, which is the most tremendous demand that may be made upon him. Nature is the third form with which we are concerned here, and as the Idea in particularity, it stands between both extremes.

This form is the most congenial to the understanding. Spirit is posited as contradiction existing for itself, for there is an objective contradiction between the Idea in its infinite freedom and in the form of singularity, which occurs in nature only as an implicit contradiction, or as a contradiction which has being for us in that otherness appears in the Idea as a stable form. In Christ the contradiction is posited and overcome as life, passion and resurrection. Nature is the Son of God, not as the Son however, but as abiding in otherness, in which the divine Idea is alienated from love and held fast for a moment. Nature is self-alienated spirit; spirit, a bacchantic god innocent of restraint and reflection has merely been *let loose* into it; in nature, the unity of the Notion conceals itself.[15]

The world, which is part of the self-disclosure of the love of God, for Hegel is also the embodiment of freedom. God is free and what he posits himself in, namely the world of history, is also free. 'It belongs to the absolute freedom of the Idea that, in its act of determining and dividing, it releases the other to exist as a free and independent being. This other, released as something free and independent is the world as such.' The doctrine of creation as the self-disclosure of God in otherness is linked by Hegel to the Incarnation, as the following passage from his *Philosophy of Nature* emphasizes:

God has two revelations, as nature and as spirit, and both manifestations are temples which He fills, and in which He is present. God as an abstraction is not the true God; His truth is the positing of His other, the living process, the world, which is His Son when it is comprehended in its divine form. God is subject only in unity with His other in spirit. The determination and the purpose of the philosophy of nature is therefore that spirit should find its own essence, its counterpart, i.e. the Notion within nature. The study of nature is therefore the liberation of what belongs to spirit within nature, for spirit is in nature in so far as it relates itself not to another, but to itself. This is likewise the liberation of nature, which in itself is reason; it is only through spirit however, that reason as such comes forth from nature into existence. Spirit has the certainty which Adam had when he beheld Eve. 'This is flesh of my flesh, this is bone of my bones.' Nature is, so to speak, the bride espoused by spirit.[16]

Incarnation

These ideas throw light upon Hegel's concept of the Incarnation in Christian thought, which he sees as a representation in religious form of the conceptual truth about the nature of God as consciousness and subjectivity. The Incarnation of God in Christ is for Hegel a historical and experimental representation of the necessity for God to be externalized in otherness in human form, with a body and with a history:

This implicit being, this implicitly subsisting unity of divine and human nature, must come to consciousness in infinite anguish – but only in accord with implicit being, with substantiality, so that finitude, weakness, and otherness can do no harm to the substantial unity of the two. Or expressed differently, the substantiality of the unity of divine and human nature comes to consciousness for humanity in such a way that a human being appears to consciousness as God, and God appears to it as human being. This is the necessity and need for such an appearance.

Furthermore, the consciousness of the absolute idea that we have in philosophy in the form of thinking is to be brought forth not for the standpoint of philosophical speculation or speculative thinking but in the form of *certainty*. The necessity [that the divine-human unity shall appear] is not first apprehended by means of thinking; rather it is a certainty for humanity. In other words, this content – the unity of divine and human nature – achieves certainty, obtaining the form of immediate sensible intuition and external existence for humankind, so that it appears as something that has been seen in the world, something that has been experienced. It is essential to this form of nonspeculative consciousness that it must be *before* us; it must essentially be *before* me – it must become a certainty for humanity. For it is only what exists in an immediate way, in inner or outer intuition, that is certain. In order for it [this divine-human unity] to become a certainty for humanity, *God had to appear in the world in the flesh* [cf. John 1:14]. The necessity that God [has] appeared in the world in the flesh is an essential characteristic – a necessary deduction from what has been said previously, demonstrated by it – for only in this way can it become a certainty for humanity; only in this way is it the truth in the form of certainty.

At the same time there is this precise specification to be added, namely, that the unity of divine and human nature must appear in *just one human being*. Humanity in itself as such is the universal, or the thought of humanity. From the present standpoint, however, it is not a question of the thought of humanity but of sensible certainty; thus it is just one human being in whom this unity is envisaged – humanity as singular, or in the determinacy of singularity and particularity. Moreover, it is not just a matter of singularity *in general*, for singularity in general is something universal once more. But from the present standpoint, singularity is not something universal; universal singularity is found in abstract thinking as such. Here, however, it is a question of the certainty of intuiting and sensing. The substantial unity [of God and humanity] is what humanity implicitly is; hence it is something that lies beyond immediate consciousness, beyond ordinary consciousness and knowledge. Hence it must stand over against subjective consciousness, which relates to itself as ordinary consciousness and is defined as such. That is exactly why the unity in question must appear for others as a singular human being set apart; it is not present in the others, but only in one from whom all the others are excluded.

Thus this one stands over against the others as what humanity implicitly is – a single individual [who is there] as the soil of certainty.[17]

But this representation is misunderstood if it is seen as

only a single event which is confined to Jesus himself. Rather the Incarnation is a represenation of how the world and human history are part of the nature of God. As Hans Küng says: 'Jesus is the revelation of that God man which is the hidden, true nature of every person.' This point is emphasized by Hegel:

> The substantial relationship of man to God *seems* to be in its truth a *beyond*, but the love of God to man and of man to God overcomes the separation of the 'Here' and the 'Now' from what is represented as a Beyond and is *eternal life*.
>
> This identity is *intuited in Christ*. As the Son of Man, he *is* the Son of God. For the God-man there is no beyond. He counts not as this *single* individual but as *universal* man, as true man. The external side of his history must be distinguished from the religious side. He has passed through the actual world, through lowliness, ignominy, has died. His *pain* was the depth of unity of the divine and the human nature in living suffering. The blessed gods of the heathens were represented as in a world beyond; through Christ, the ordinary actual world, this *lowliness* which is not contemptible, is *itself hallowed*.[18]

Indeed Hegel uses the term *Lebenslauf* or 'career' to indicate what he means here: that God develops subjectivity and consciousness through Incarnation in otherness generally, not just in Christ, and that this insight when it is understood and comprehended in all its natural and historical detail in philosophy leads to Absolute Knowing or Absolute Spirit, which again is represented in religious terms by the doctrine of the Holy Spirit:

> This individual man, then, which absolute Being has revealed itself to be, accomplishes in himself as an individual the movement of sensuous Being. He is the *immediately* present God; consequently, his '*being*' passes over into '*having been*'. Consciousness, for which God is thus sensuously present, ceases to see and to hear Him; it *has* seen and heard Him; and it is because it only *has* seen and heard Him that it first becomes itself spiritual consciousness. Or, in other words, just as formerly He rose up for consciousness as a *sensuous* existence, now He has arisen *in the Spirit*. For a consciousness that sensuously sees and hears Him is itself a merely immediate consciousness, which has not overcome the disparity of objectivity, has not taken it back into pure thought: it knows this objective individual, but not itself, as Spirit. In the vanishing of the immediate existence known to be absolute Being the immediacy receives its negative moment; Spirit remains the immediate Self of actuality, but as the *universal self-consciousness* of the [religious] community, a self-consciousness which reposes in its own substance, just as in it this Substance is a universal Subject: not the individual by himself, but together with the consciousness of the community and what he is for this community, is the complete whole of the individual as Spirit.[19]

Spirit is thus posited in the third element, in *universal self-consciousness*; it is its *community*. The movement of

41

the community as self-consciousness that has distinguished itself from its picture-thought is to make explicit
what has been implicitly established. The dead divine
Man or human God is *in himself* the universal self-
consciousness. Or, since this self-consciousness consti-
tutes one side of the antithesis in picture-thought, viz.
The side of evil, for which natural existence and
individual self-consciousness count as essence – this side
which is pictured as independent, not yet as a moment,
has on account of its independence to raise itself
through its own nature to Spirit, i.e. it has to exhibit in
its own self the movement of Spirit.[20]

So Hegel regards his philosophy as providing an interpretation of the doctrine of the Trinity, a point which is made
clear in the following passage from the *Philosophy of
Religion*.

The first moment is the idea in its simple universality for
itself, self-enclosed, having not yet progressed to the
primal division, to otherness – the Father. The second is
the particular, the idea in appearance – the Son. It is the
idea in its externality, such that the external appearance
is converted back to the first [moment] and is known as
the divine idea, the identity of the divine and the
human. The third element, then, is this consciousness –
God as the Spirit. The Spirit as existing and realizing itself
is the community.[21]

This idea, that the doctrine of the Trinity is closely linked to
the notion of community in Christian belief, is one which
many theologians after Hegel have developed.

The Fall

Again Hegel gives a philosophical transcription of the religious representation of the Fall of man in the Garden of Eden which, Hegel holds, tells us a deep truth about the nature of human existence.

This accordingly is the mode and manner of the shape in which this conceptual determination appears representationally as a story and is represented for consciousness in an intuitable or sensible mode, so that it is regarded as something that *happened*. It is the familiar story in Genesis. The gist of it is that God created human beings in his own image: this is the concept of the human being. Humankind lived in Paradise; we can call it a zoological garden. This life is called the state of innocence. The story says, too, that the tree of the knowledge of good and evil stood in Paradise, and that human beings disobeyed God's command by eating of it. On the one hand, it is formally set down that this eating was the transgression of a commandment. The content, however, is the essential thing, namely, that the sin consisted in having eaten of the tree of knowledge of good and evil, and in this connection there comes about the pretense of the serpent that humanity will be like God when it has the knowledge of good and evil.

It is said, then, that human beings have eaten of this tree. It is clear, as far as the content is concerned, that the fruit is an outward image – it belongs only to the sensible portrayal. What it really means is that humanity has elevated itself to the knowledge of good and evil; and this cognition, this distinction, is the source of evil, is evil itself. Being evil is located in the act of cognition, in consciousness. And certainly, as we already said earlier, being evil resides in the cognitive knowledge; cognition is the source of evil. For cognition or consciousness means in general a judging or dividing, a self-distinguishing within oneself. Animals have no consciousness, they are unable to make distinctions within themselves, they have no free being-for-self in the face of objectivity generally. The cleavage, however, is what is evil; it is the contradiction. It contains the two sides: good and evil. Only in this cleavage is evil contained, and hence it is itself evil. Therefore it is entirely correct to say that good and evil are first to be found in consciousness.

The first human being is represented as having brought about this fall. Here again we have this sensible mode of expression. From the point of view of thought, the expression 'the first human being' signifies 'humanity itself' or 'humanity as such' – not some single, contingent individual, not one among many, but the absolutely first one, humanity according to its concept. Human being as such is conscious being; it is precisely for that reason that humanity enters into this cleavage, into the consciousness that, when it is further specified, is cognition. But inasmuch as universal humanity is represented as a first man, he is represented as distinguished from others. Hence the question arises: if there is only one who has done this, how is that deed transmitted to others? Here the notion of inheritance of sin that is passed on to all others comes into play. By this means the deficiency involved in viewing humanity as such representationally as a first man is corrected. The one-sidedness involved in representing the cleavage belonging to the concept of human being generally as the act of a single individual is absorbed by this notion of a communicated or inherited sin. Neither the original representation nor the correction are really necessary; for it is humanity as a whole that, as consciousness, enters into this cleavage.[22]

The Garden of Eden story represents the innocence of humanity in a kind of unmediated unity with the divine and with nature, but humanity in such circumstances is not aware of its own subjectivity and spirit. Eating of the tree of knowledge gives man knowledge of good and evil, it gives him a sense that for good or ill he can follow his own path. It is the birth of individualism and personal responsibility. This unmediated unity is broken and man seeks through all the modes of experience which Hegel describes in his philosophy to realize his individual nature in many diverse ways. But again, the Christian religion represents the possibility of redemption, of a return not to a prelapsarian state of innocence and unmediated unity, but, philosophically understood, to a new kind of mediated unity when we understand things from the point of view of Absolute Knowledge in which all the gains of human individuality, which would not have been possible if humanity had stayed in the mythological Garden of Eden, are preserved and integrated into this new philosophical vision. So again we have to transcend the representational in the story in Genesis and transcribe the story into a philosophical form, that reintegration of humanity is possible but only by the struggle entailed in the philosophical comprehension of the totality of our historical experience as human beings:

> From the point of view of thought, the expression 'the first human being' signifies 'humanity in itself' or 'humanity as such' not some single contingent individual (i.e. Adam RP), not one among many, but the absolutely first one, humanity according to its concept. Human being as such is a conscious being; it is precisely for that reason that humanity enters into this cleavage ... But in the same way as this cleavage is the source of evil, it is also the mid point of the conversion that consciousness contains within itself whereby this cleavage is also sublated.[23]

Individual consciousness thus leads for Hegel to the capacity for right and wrong but because consciousness also has the primordial desire for unity as Hegel has maintained throughout his work, the possibility for overcoming the Fall, and the diremption that it causes, could be overcome by consciousness itself and thus, in his language 'this cleavage is sublated'.

Redemption comes through the philosophical grasp of the totality of human experience which would not have been possible without the Fall. Redemption does not restore 'innocence to the fallen' as the *Praeconium Paschale* says because there can be no return to innocence. What we seek now is for Hegel a mediated unity in which the totality of experience is gathered together, but this is a struggle – as he says in *Phenomenology of Spirit* – it is the 'Golgotha of Absolute Spirit'.

Religion and Philosophy

Little more remains to be said about the relationship between religion and philosophy. They are both modes of Absolute Knowledge but philosophy transcends religion which gets caught up on stories and representation which can lead to the forms of bifurcation which, as we saw, were central concerns at the Stift:

> Since what is at issue is the consciousness of absolute reconciliation, we are here in the presence of a new consciousness of humanity or a new religion. Through it a new world is constituted, a new actuality, a different world-condition, because [humanity's] outward determinate being, [its] natural existence, now has religion as its substantiality. This is the aspect that is negative and polemical, being opposed to the subsistence of externality in the consciousness of humanity. The new religion expresses itself precisely as a new consciousness, the consciousness of a reconciliation of humanity with God. This reconciliation, expressed as a state of affairs, is the kingdom of God, an actuality. The souls and hearts [of individuals] are reconciled with God, and thus it is God who rules in the heart and has attained dominion.[24]

So if we say now that philosophy ought to consider religion, then these two are likewise set in a relationship of distinction in which they stand in opposition to one another. But on the contrary it must be said that the content of philosophy, its need and interest, is wholly in common with that of religion. The object of religion, like that of philosophy, is the eternal truth, God and nothing but God and the explication of God. Philosophy is only explicating *itself* when it explicates religion, and when it explicates itself it is explicating religion. For the *thinking* spirit is what penetrates this object, the truth; it is thinking that enjoys the truth and purifies the subjective consciousness. Thus religion and philosophy coincide in one. In fact philosophy is itself the service of God, as is religion. But each of them, religion as well as philosophy, is the service of God in a way peculiar to it (about which more needs to be said). They differ in the peculiar character of their concern with God. This is where the difficulties lie that impede philosophy's grasp of religion; and it often appears impossible for the two of them to be united. The apprehensive attitude of religion toward philosophy and the hostile stance of each toward the other arise from this. It seems, as the theologians frequently suggest, that philosophy works to corrupt the content of religion, destroying and profaning it. This old antipathy stands before our eyes as something admitted and acknowledged, more generally acknowledged than their unity. The time seems to have arrived, however, when philosophy can deal with religion more impartially on the one hand, and more fruitfully and auspiciously on the other.[25]

The fact that the religious content is present primarily in the form of representation is connected with what I said earlier, that religion is the consciousness of absolute truth in the way that it occurs for all human beings. Thus it is found primarily in the form of representation. Philosophy has the same content, the truth; it is the spirit of the world generally and not the particular spirit.

Philosophy does nothing but transform our representations into concepts. The content remains always the same.[26]

Philosophy is, as Hegel says in his *Lectures on the Philosophy of Religion*, '*Gottes dienst*' – the service of God. The transcription of human life and history into philosophical concepts and set within a total explanation which is Absolute Knowledge is a transcription of the nature and history of God. It puts the content of religion in a new way so that we do not apprehend the deep truths of our lives only through stories and representations but also through a conceptual structure which is publicly available to all, and as a shared understanding of experience can form the basis of a common life.

This reconciliation is philosophy. Philosophy is to this extent theology. It presents the reconciliation of God with himself and with nature, showing that nature, otherness, is implicitly divine, and that the raising of itself to reconciliation is on the other hand what finite spirit implicitly is, while on the other hand it arrives at this reconciliation, or brings it forth, in world history. This reconciliation is the peace of God, which does not 'surpass all reason', but is rather the peace that *through* reason is first known and thought and is recognized as what is true.[27]

CONCLUSION

For Hegel, therefore, the philosophy of religion is not just a specific branch of philosophy dealing with a specific set of intellectual problems within religion. It is much more profound and pervasive than that. The Christian religion, properly understood, provides us with an integrated account of human existence both historically and in the modern world. It is for Hegel the basis for a new humanity when it is philosophically transcribed and comprehended. As he says in *The Phenomenology of Spirit*, philosophy becomes the foundation for an 'accomplished community of consciousness' and thus the basis for a common life. For Hegel, then, the task of philosophy is not just the elaboration of sets of general principles, but is rooted in our personal, social and cultural experience, providing an interpretation of what is and through this interpretation transforming and transfiguring it. A pervasive part of this experience is directly involved in religion and that which may appear at the level of the Understanding not to be can be seen from the standpoint of Absolute Knowledge to be capable of being understood in terms of appropriately rethought Christian categories. Thus, having seen Christianity initially as part of the problem of fragmentation in the modern world, it becomes in his mature thought the basic part of the solution and it does this by changing and developing our understanding of the nature of God, Incarnation, Holy Spirit and the Trinity.

Hegel's theology is best characterized by the term 'panen-theism' which usefully distinguishes his views from deism, pantheism and orthodox theism. Hegel clearly rejects enlightenment deism in terms of which God creates the universe, but has no further role within it. It is different from the pantheism of Spinoza in whose work God is identified with the world as a whole. This is because for Hegel we cannot treat the given world as identical with God any more than we can treat a person as identical with a list of his bodily parts. The world, natural, personal, social, political and cultural, is transfigured by the self-revelation of God within it. So as a person has a body and could not be a person without one, nevertheless a person is not reducible to a description of the body. Hegel's philosophy is not pantheistic because we do have a conception of God as he is in himself (the Absolute Idea) but this knowledge of God is abstract without an understanding of the self-positing of God in the world which has to occur if God is to consciousness and Spirit. Equally, for reasons that I have already given, Hegel's work is at odds with orthodox Christian theism. Against Hegel's claim that without the world God would not be God, the world of orthodoxy would take the contrary view that the being and nature of God has to be understood independently of the world. For Hegel, however, God is not just 'in himself' but also 'for himself' as embodied in the world. So panentheism, which was a term coined by Krause, a philosophical contemporary of Hegel's, seems to be the best way of categorizing Hegel's understanding of religion. Panentheism is made up of three Greek words: *pan* meaning all or everything, *en* meaning in, *theos* meaning God and it is intended to convey precisely what Hegel meant: that God is immanent in the world but is more than the sum of the parts of the world.

Hegel's religious thought, as I have described it, became very influential in the latter part of the nineteenth century, particularly in Britain through its impact on T.H. Green, Sir Henry Jones and John and Edward Caird. It was so influential for two related reasons. First of all Green and his colleagues were very taken with the idea that Hegel's philosophy, providing as it did an account of how human common life could be achieved by this common understanding of the Christian basis of civilization. This was a point made particularly well by Green in his sermon 'The Word is Nigh Thee':

> If there is an essence within the essence of Christianity, it is the thought embodied in the text I have read; the thought of God not as far off but 'nigh'; not as master but as father; not as terrible outward power forcing us we know not whither, but as one whom we may say that we are reason of his reason, and spirit of his spirit, who lives in our moral life and for whom we live in living for the brethren and in so living we live freely.[28]

Understood in this way, Christianity could become the basis of a common life.

The second reason why it became so influential was that it was thought that Hegel's philosophy of religion provided materials for the defence of Christianity against two intellectual currents of the generations which followed Hegel, namely: the historical critique of the life of Jesus, and the development of the theory of evolution. The development of the historical critique of the life of Jesus, particularly in the hands of Strauss who was much influenced by Hegel, posed major problems for later nineteenth-century Christian thinkers and yet Hegel's philosophy, just because it detached a proper understanding of the nature of Christianity from the particular figure of Jesus, made it possible to mount a defence of Christianity which was largely immune from this kind of historical critique. As Green wrote:

> At a time when every thoughtful man accustomed to call himself a Christian is asking the faith he professes for some account of its origins and authority, it is a pity the answer should be confused by the habit of identifying Christianity with the set of written propositions which constitute the New Testament.

Since Christianity could be understood philosophically, it could be made relatively immune to this form of historically based attack on the details of the Gospels' account of the life of Jesus.

In addition, because Hegel had stressed the self-developmental of God in the world of nature and culture, it was thought by some British Hegelians, particularly J. R. Illingworth, that a Hegelianized form of Christianity could be made compatible with the theory of evolution as a developmental account of nature. This is not the place to go into the extent to which this kind of account of Christianity could achieve these goals, but certainly the possibility seemed to be there for those who were influenced by this work.

Hegel's work poses a considerable challenge to modern thought in several respects. To the Christian thinker it raises the question of the nature of orthodoxy and whether his account of the nature of God and the other doctrines that flow from that can be accommodated within something recognizably Christian and, if it can, how these ideas might be rethought in a more contemporary idiom. Those who have made the most progress on this are probably on the one hand the Process theologians who follow in the footsteps of A. N. Whitehead and C. Hatshorne. Although there are some significant differences between Process philosophers and Hegel, nevertheless there is a large degree of overlap and their thought provides the best modern account of how a developmental metaphysic of the sort adopted by Hegel might be made salient to modern sensibilities. Hegel also poses a general challenge for contemporary religious thought in the sense that if one is a Christian and one holds that Christianity as a religion of incarnation provides some general and universal truths about human existence, how are these truths to be understood in detail in relation to the world as it is shown to be by modern natural and social science and history? Modern theologians have sometimes paid lip service to the need for a comprehensive account of religious thought in this sense, but there is precious little in detail to show for it in terms of providing a unifying perspective on human existence in the way that Hegel thought was indispensable and which he struggled to achieve. Yet from a Christian perspective, if this religion makes universal claims not just about private and personal relationships but about the natural world in which we exist and the forms of culture and community which we build to make sense of that existence, then however flawed Hegel's own vision may be the demand for comprehensiveness which he articulated, not just as an intellectual demand, but one which could form the basis of a common life, remains to be met in our age.

The other major challenge that Hegel's work poses to modern Christian theology can perhaps best be thought of in terms of the contrast with the currently popular narrative theology. Narrative theology shares with a good deal of post-modern philosophy a scepticism about the role of reason and metaphysics within religion. There is no general form of reason which could yield the comprehensive system which Hegel's thought embodies. Reason is internal to specific communities which are shaped by narrative, common interests and common traditions. What is rational and irrational is internal to different narratives whether these be the narratives of Christianity or something else. There is, however, no general, comprehensive, rational system or meta narrative which could, as Hegel tried to do through his account of dialectic, place particular narratives within a more general framework. The narrative theologies associated with S. Hauerwas and J. MacLendon not only share the scepticism of a general account of reason that is not related to narrative and tradition, they also believe that from a Christian perspective such a commitment to a general view of reason would be positively harmful to the nature of Christianity. If we had a comprehensive account of reason of the sort that Hegel tries to provide, then, they argue, the narrative form of Christianity would become a kind of illustration or embellishment of truths that could be known on other grounds which, in a sense, is precisely what Hegel tried to do with his transformation of Christianity. These points however take us back to where we started with Hegel who was, as we saw, profoundly concerned with the fragmentation of the common life of society and the fragmentation of the self which was unable to achieve a comprehensive interpretation of existence. If there is no general account of the nature of human life and purpose and no meta narrative, only specific narratives based upon faith and commitment, then we run the risk of a very polarized world in which people belong to their particular narratively formed communities with no sense of common purposes and common life. Hegel's life's work was devoted to showing the dangers in such an approach and, through his philosophy, that it was not necessary.

NOTES

1. Nohl, H. (ed.), *Hegel's Theologische Jugendschriften* (Mohr, Tübingen, 1907), p. 245.

2. Ibid., p. 27.

3. Ibid., p. 28.

4. Ibid., p. 333.

5. Mackinnon, D., *The Borderlands of Theology* (Lutterworth, London, 1968), p. 83

6. Hegel, G.L.F., *The Earliest System – Programme of German Idealism*, translated as an Appendix to H.S. Harris's *Hegel's Development Towards the Sunlight* (The Clarendon Press, Oxford, 1972), p. 511.

7. Glockner, H. (ed.), *Hegel's Sämtliche Werke*, Vol. X, (frommann-holzboog, Stuttgart, 1965) p. 259.

8. Hampshire, S.N., *Thought and Action* (Jonathan Cape, London, 1959), p. 276.

9. Hegel, G.W.F., *The Phenomenology of Spirit*, trans. A.V. Miller (The Clarendon Press, Oxford, 1977), p. 493.

10. Hegel, G.W.F., *Lectures on the Philosophy of Religion*, ed. P. Hodgson (University of California Press, Berkeley/Los Angeles/London, 1988), p. 473.

11. Eliot, T.S., 'Little Gidding', in *Collected Poems 1909–1962* (Faber & Faber, London, 1963), p. 222.

12. Hegel, G.W.F., *Lectures on the Philosophy of Religion*, Vol. I, ed. P. Hodgson (University of California Press, Berkeley/Los Angeles/London 1984), pp. 126–7.

13. Hegel, G.W.F., *The Philosophy of Nature*, ed. M.J. Petry (George Allen & Unwin, London, 1970), Vol. I, p. 205.

14. Hegel, G.W.F., *Lectures on the Philosophy of Religion*, Vol. I, op. cit., p. 381.

15. Hegel, G.W.F., *Philosophy of Nature*, Vol. I, op. cit., p. 205.

16. Ibid., p. 204.

17. Hegel, G.W.F., *Lectures on the Philosophy of Religion*, one-volume edition, (University of California Press, Berkeley/Los Angeles/London, 1988) op. cit., p. 454.

18. Hegel, G.W.F., *The Philosophical Propaedeutic*, ed. A. Vincent and M. George (Blackwells, Oxford, 1986), p. 168.

19. Hegel, G.W.F., *The Phenomenology of Spirit*, op. cit., p. 462.

20. Ibid., p. 473.

21. Hegel, G.W.F., *Lectures on the Philosophy of Religion*, one-volume edition, op. cit., p. 473.

22. Ibid., p. 442.

23. Ibid.

24. Ibid., p. 459.

25. Ibid., p. 78.

26. Ibid.

27. Ibid., p. 489.

28. Green, T.H., *Collected Works*, vol. 3 (Longman Green, London, 1885), p. 221.